CROW!

CROW!

The Children's Poems

by Steven R. Cope

Illustrations by Julie Baumgardner

WIND PUBLICATIONS

 For information address Wind Publications, 600 Overbrook Drive, Nicholasville, KY 40356.

First edition.

International Standard Book Number 1893239365
Library of Congress Control Number 2004114074

Other Works by Steven R. Cope

In Killdeer's Field
Sassafras
The Book Of Saws
Clover's Log
The Year Of Mahler's 9th
demi-poems
Standin' Right Here (Music, CD)
Rubber Room (Music, CD)
FrogVille (DVD Animation Series, Niolan Entertainment, Belgium)

Acknowledgments

Thanks to the editors of *Northern Stars Magazine* where early versions of some of these poems first appeared . . . and to Kitty H. and Jay Jay M. and Kathy M. and Linda H. and Vaughn J. and Ronnie H. and Tommy H. and John S. and Bobby C. and David C. and Julie C. and O.V.S. and Steve S. and Marcus M. and Brenda M. and Cheryl C. and Carlos C. and Mark H. and Mike H. and Carolyn H. and Mickey C. and Cliff S. and Diane S. and Bob H. and Bud H. and Jerry W. and Sandy N. and Mary Lou N. and Victor T. and Vernon T. and David P. and Louie B. and Lois B. and Pam C. and Cassie C. and Ellen C. and Janet C. and Jennifer C. and Nancy H. and Judith B. and Lisa S. and Ricky S., all of whom shall remain forever young. Thanks also to D.D. for his latter-day inspiration.

The illustrator, Julie Baumgardner resides in Winchester, Kentucky, with her husband and son. She has taught visual art in the public schools for 18 years. This is the second of Cope's books that contain her illustrations.

I'm just an old crow, you can see—
But what else would I want to be?
SRC

To Cori, John Allen, & Daniel

Introduction

To Steven R. Cope both the prompting and the desire to write came from the land, from the mysterious east Kentucky hills of Menifee County where he was born. But it also came from his beloved kinfolk, particularly his grandmother Eunice Gose Cope. "She was an amazing woman who never forgot anything she had learned," Steve said, "spoke meticulous English, was a piano player, and once a school teacher." Many of his relatives, particularly the female, at one time or another were teachers, and though Steve was not so much encouraged to write, he was always encouraged to read. Along with his basketball and baseball glove, his tiny 20-gauge shotgun (which had belonged to his Uncle Forrest, missing in action since World War II), he prized his books over all his possessions. "My childhood could not have been more perfect, unified, harmonious. And yet I knew from my close proximity to nature that everything was so terribly fleeting. I began writing, I think, more to preserve the past than anything else." In later years Steve's writing has become for him a search, an attempt to discover again that kind of unity and coherence which life seemed to have in his youth. Like *The Book of Saws*, this complete collection of children's poems shows another side of Steven Cope, a playful side, a joyous side that offsets the deep seriousness of much of his other work.

Contents

— The Poems —

About A Book

About a book
There's much to say;
This one's meant
To last all day.

I wrote it all
Without a map,
With a kitten
On my lap,

With my birds
At my right ear
Wondering what
I'm doing here,

With my hat
Upon my head,
My 6-string silent
On my bed.

I wrote it cause
When I was small
And tried to
Understand it all

A book would
Take me everywhere
And I'd be glad
The book was there.

Ain't Is Not A Word

Ain't is not a word
So maybe when Aunt Ginny
Said I ain't got much,
She meant I haven't many.

And So And So Forth . . .

And So and So Forth . . .
One went south, the other north.

One wore plaid, one wore jeans,
One ate beets, the other beans.

One wore a coat, one a sweater,
One wrote a book, one a letter.

One wore sideburns, one was shaved,
One got lost, the other saved.

One had lunch, one had dinner,
One got fat, the other thinner.

One jammed his thumb, one his toe,
One had to stay, the other go.

One got up, one sat down,
One walked in, one walked around.

One kissed a frog, one a turtle,
One jumped the gun, one a hurdle.

One did quite well, the other failed,
One stayed on board, the other bailed.

One lost the race, one didn't run it,
One did it all, one wished he'd done it.

And so And So and So Forth died
And never once stood side by side.

Animals Are People

Animals are people
With legs and a tail,
But instead of a sidewalk
They have a trail,

But instead of a house
They have a den,
But instead of a wife
They have a hen,

But instead of a nail
They have a claw,
But instead of a hand
They have a paw,

But instead of a sweater
They have a coat,
But instead of a word
They have a note,

But instead of a nose
They have a beak,
But instead of a bathtub
They have a creek,

But instead of a bed
They have a log,
But instead of a pool
They have a bog,

But instead of a shirt
They have a feather,
But instead of a lawn
They have a heather,

But instead of a grumble
They have a growl,
But instead of a cheer
They have a howl,

But instead of a motel
They have a zoo,
But instead of a crowd
They have a slew,

But instead of a child
They have a chick,
But instead of a board
They have a stick,

But instead of a club
They have a sty,
But instead of a church
They have a sky,

But instead of a sewer
They have a stream,
But instead of a movie
They have a dream,

But instead of a plan
They have a way,
But instead of a future
They have a day.

An Owl Said "Whooo!"

An owl said "Whooo!"
And turned his head
And made as if to
Make his bed;

And then he heard
From down below
A squeaky voice
So very low.

"Not I," it said,
And then a pause,
And then a bigger
Thing with claws.

"Not I," it growled,
And then aloud
A chorus upstairs
In a cloud,

"Not I."
"Not I."
"Not I."
"Not I."

And on the ground
All through the trees
Fell other creatures
To their knees:

"Not I."
"Not I."
"Not I."
"Not I."

Then "Whoooooo???"
The owl said once again
And pulled the covers
To his chin.

Anyone That Has An Eye

Anyone that has an eye
Ought to see a pig fly by,
And ought to see a goat and fox,
And then a sack and then a box;

And then a can and then a wrapper,
And then a pioneer and trapper,
And then an entire generation,
And then a country and a nation.

Anyone that has another
Ought to see his great-grandmother,
Rocking in her rocking chair
And sailing off into the air.

Autumn Was A Teensy Thing

Autumn was a teensy thing
No more than two feet high,
With dimples on her everywhere
And chocolate in her eye.

And Logan was a little squirrel
Who liked to shake his tail
When Autumn walked out on the porch
Or ran to get the mail.

And up a tree the squirrel would zip
When Autumn threw her shoe;
Such chattering was never heard
Outside of a zoo.

The Balloon Man Is Coming!

The balloon man is coming!
I can hardly wait.
He'll be there at seven
And I will not be late.
My pockets are loaded
With nickels and dimes,
Wadded up baseball cards,
Lemons and limes;
I'll buy and I'll trade
For a dozen balloons,
All painted with faces
And silly cartoons,
And when I am through
I'll go out in the yard,
And I'll take off running
So fast and so hard
That all of a sudden
I'll come up off my feet
And go sailing in air
Way up over the street.
And people will point
And say "Look way up there!"
And *I'll* be the balloon man
At the Clark County Fair.

Be Great, Spot

Be great, Spot,
Cause you know how—
By doing what
You can do now.

Don't think too much
Of what you might
Like to do
Some other night.

Don't plan too great
A plan just yet;
Don't try to dig
Where it's too wet.

Just do today
What you can do
And let the bones
All come to you.

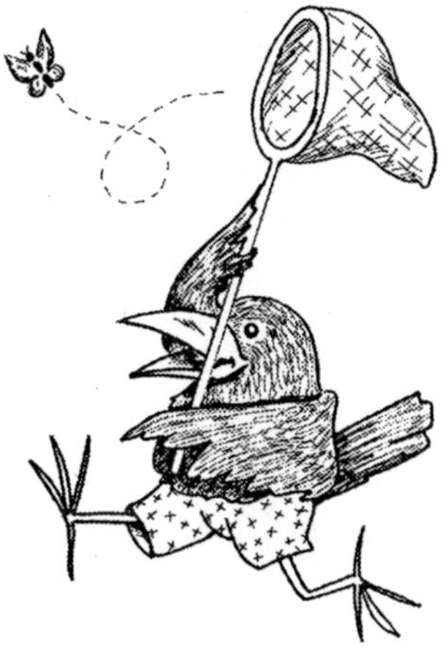

The Best Is Yet To Be

The best is yet to be,
Cried a chigger to a flea,
A flock of dogs is headed right toward gee!

And close behind them there's a goose
And to his left there is a moose
And a herd of chickens headed right toward gee!

And up above there is a cloud
Of honeybees a-barkin loud
And a gaggle of opossums headed toward gee!

I would not move a stitch
If you want them all to itch,
There's a pride of turkeys headed right toward gee!

Stay right there where you are,
They're a-comin wide and far,
There's a school of monkeys headed right toward gee!

And behind them is a clutch
Of polar bears and such
And a pod of pilgrims headed right toward gee!

Birds Sing Of Course Which I Declare

Birds sing of course which I declare
Makes life so lovely in the air.

I can't jump up off my feet
Without I hear them go tweet, tweet.

Tweet, tweet! there they go!
Can you hear them down below?

I would tell you what I heard
But I can't sing it like a bird.

A Blue Ball Is Not A Red Ball

A blue ball is not a red ball,
That I can swear,
But how do you tell
The difference there?

Does one bounce high
And one bounce low?
Is one better suited
For George or Joe?

Or does one roll off
While the other rolls on?
Or does one float better
In my daddy's pond?

Does one like sunlight,
One like rain,
One bounce off
A windowpane?

Will one konk better
Somebody's head?
Will one get lost
Beneath my bed?

Is one for girls?
One for boys?
Will one blend in
With my other toys?

Sometimes I don't know
What to do.
Which do I want—
The red or blue?

A Bony Old Pony

A bony old pony,
A skinny old cow—
Won't somebody feed you
Or don't they know how?

If you lived at my house
You'd be fat as shoats—
On ice cream and cookies
And butterscotch oats.

Bubba Grew A Beard

Bubba grew a beard
All over his chin
Till it looked like a mouse
That the cat dragged in

Or a nest of pimples
In a big pink tree . . .
But don't tell Bubba,
He'll clobber me!

Bubbles, Bubbles Everywhere

Bubbles, bubbles everywhere,
Bubbles on my nose,
Bubbles in my earlobe,
Bubbles on my toes,

Bubbles in my navel,
Bubbles on my knee,
Everywhere I've got a spot
Bubbles cover me.

Bubbles in the tree tops,
Bubbles on the cat,
Bubbles on the goldfish,
Bubbles on the rat,

Bubbles on the raccoon,
Bubbles on the pup,
Everywhere there is a hole
Bubbles fill it up.

Yellow bubbles, blue bubbles,
Bubbles every hue,
Bubbles in the factory,
Bubbles in the zoo,

Bubbles at the ballpark,
Bubbles at the school,
Bubbles in the fountain,
Bubbles at the pool,

Big bubbles, little bubbles,
Bubbles every size,
Bubbles with a mustache,
Bubbles in disguise.

Bubbles wearing blue jeans,
Bubbles wearing shirts,
Hula, hula bubbles
In their bubble skirts,

Bubbles with a hat on,
Bubbles with a beard,
Bubbles on my bubbles—
Now that is really weird!

Buck Rode A Horse

Buck rode a horse
Which wasn't too strange
But he rode that horse
On a driving range

And a golf ball hit him
Right between the eyes
And then something else
To his surprise:

A gopher ran out
To kick the horse's knee
And the horse bucked Buck
Up in a tree

And he commenced to crowing
Till the moon arose
And a coon hunter shot him
Right between the nose.

A Bug Is Little

A bug is little.
A little bug is really little.
And even if its ear is red
It's hard to see it on its head.

A Bull Bit A Baker

A bull bit a baker
In the back of his behind
When the baker bent down
Beneath a bonbon vine,

And the baker was as huffy
As a big sweet roll
But the bull grinned as round
As a donut hole.

Calico River's Bout Two Feet Long

Calico River's bout two feet long
With a puddle in the middle and a green ping pong,
And fourteen chippers in a dead pine tree
Sing get this truck tire off of me!

Calico River's bout two feet wide
With a tin can mountain on the other side,
And a great big pimple on its mud-banked chin
And a milk jug floating on the other end.

Calico River's bout two feet tall
And comes up to your waist at the waterfall
And up to your neck if it rains dead frogs
And up to your eyes if it rains fat hogs.

Calico River's bout two feet deep,
So lovely from the air it makes you weep,
But don't dive in, you'll crack your head
On the rusty old stove in the river bed.

Cantaloupe, Antelope, Rodeo, Gold

Cantaloupe, antelope, rodeo, gold—
Some words march right down the road.

Stop! Whoa! Halt! Quit!—
Must be words at the end of it.

A Catcher Of Fishes

A catcher of fishes,
A keeper of bees,
My Papaw played dominoes
Down on his knees.

Cats Are Cool

Cats are cool
And they don't care
Who it is
That's standing there.

They just stretch
And lick their fur,
Not caring if
It's him or her.

And even if
A president
Walks right up
So confident,

They might blink
Or they might not,
Cause cats still know
What we forgot.

Centipede,Centipede, What You Gonna Do

Centipede, centipede, what you gonna do
Wid all dim legs dar under you?
Sometimes I trip and I oney got two—
I'd bust my brump if I had a few!

Charles Henry Hooked A Bass Named Frank

Charles Henry hooked a bass named Frank
While fishing from a muddy bank
And that bass took off and Charles Henry's feet
Went sailing up above his seat
And Splatt! he landed on his rear
All tangled in his fishing gear
And old Frank just floated up to grin
And took off swimming hard again.

Charles Henry thought he'd hooked a whale
But he had faith he would prevail
Until that bass gave another yank
And pulled Charles Henry off the bank
And the waves were roaring like a July flood
And Charles Henry's mouth was full of mud
And old Frank just floated up to grin
And took off swimming hard again.

Charles Henry prayed like Jonah might,
Lord, give me strength for this here fight!
If I don't get some sort of traction,
I'll need another course of action.
So round and round the lake they went
Till it seemed the fish's strength was spent
But old Frank just floated up to grin
And took off swimming hard again.

A day and a night, a night and day,
He dragged Charles Henry around that way
Until one of them said, Let's take a break!
I'm tired of going round this lake!
So that's what they did for an hour or two
And Charles Henry thought the thing was through
But old Frank just floated up to grin
And took off swimming hard again.

A Clown Is A Clown But A Clown

A clown is a clown but a clown,
When nobody else is around,
Sometimes is sad
And sometimes so mad
He just needs a hug to calm down.
But that makes him no less a clown.

Cori, Oh Cori

Cori, oh Cori,
Please tell me a story
About how it used to be

When froggies had wings
Among other things
And loved to sip sassafras tea.

And tell me of crows
With rings on their toes
And top hats all white and shiny

And all sorts of wabbits
With all sorts of dag-nab-its
And a powder puff on their behiny.

And tell me of coons
With bright red balloons
And noses lit up like a cherry

And a chickadee tub
And a teddy bear cub
That grinned all the way to Combs Ferry.

Cousin Gary's More Hairy

Cousin Gary's more hairy
Than Clifton or Ed,
Got more hair on his back
Than they do on their head.

I guess that means something
But I don't know what—
Except that some have
What some others have not.

Cowboys Like To Cor-ral Cows

Cowboys like to cor-ral cows
And they can't wait to kiss the gals,
Cause gals smell good and most cows don't
And cowboys kiss and most cows won't.

Crickets Are Better Than Wickets

Crickets are better than wickets
Cause wickets cannot sing,
But you can't knock a croquet ball
Through a cricket for anything.

Crow! Crow! Crow! Crow!

Crow! Crow! Crow! Crow!
Crow! Crow! Crow!
What is that a-crowin?
Does anybody know?

I've heard chickens cluckin,
And I've heard owls go hoot,
But I've never heard such crowin
Since I was just a toot.

Crow! Said The Daddy

Crow! said the daddy,
When the chick stood still.
Crow! Crow! from way down deep in your craw!
Don't let nobody tell you
You can't twitter like no sparrow.
You're a crow, boy, a crow—so crow!

Crow! said the mama,
When the chick gave a whimper.
Crow! Crow! from way down deep in your soul!
Don't think you gotta warble
When you ain't no songbird.
You're a crow, child, a crow—so crow!

Dandelion, Oh Magic Flower

Dandelion, oh magic flower
That pea brains call a weed,

Reflect the stars upon the field
And be so honeybeed

That all the gardens of the world
Will wonder how you do it

And every connoisseur will ask
Which artist was it drew it.

Dan'l Bum Had An Uncle

Dan'l Bum had an uncle
As poor as could be.
He lived on a limb
In a sycamore tree.
And when Dan'l would visit
They'd watch the TV
While hung by their heels
Most precariously.

And Dan'l would swing
And his uncle would sway
(It's thought that real monkeys
Behave the same way),
And sometimes they'd sing
And sometimes they'd play,
Then Dan'l'd hop home
At the end of the day.

Da'od, I Saved A Crow

Da'od, I saved a crow
Right smack dab in the road,
But why the thing was really there
Nobody really knowed.

There wudn't ary corn tree
For many miles around,
But there it was as big as life—
We almost runned it down!

Da'od, Da'od,
What a sight it were,
And though you won't believe me,
It really did occur.

Denny Had A Pinhead

Denny had a pinhead
Sitting on his neck,
And every time his hat dropped down,
Denny'd say oh heck!

I asked him where he got it.
He said as a kid
He wore a rubber head-band
Tighter than a lid.

A Dog Is A Dog And A Cat Is A Cat

A dog is a dog and a cat is a cat,
But what in the world is an elephat?

And why does its eyes go round and round,
And why does its nose hang to the ground?

And how does it eat with its teeth sticking out?
And what in the world are those ears about?

Its legs are so long they reach the earth;
I wonder if those things give birth?!!

Eight Green Turtles On A Bed

Eight green turtles on a bed.
One fell off and the others said,
Would you please not shake the bed, Ed,
Would you please not shake the bed?

Seven green turtles on a bed.
One fell off and the others said,
Would you please not shake the bed, Fred,
Would you please not shake the bed?

Six green turtles on a bed.
One fell off and the others said,
Would you please not shake the bed, Ted,
Would you please not shake the bed?

Five green turtles on a bed
One fell off and the others said,
Would you please not shake the bed, Ned,
Would you please not shake the bed?

Four green turtles on a bed.
One fell off and the others said,
Would you please not shake the bed, Red,
Would you please not shake the bed?

Three green turtles on a bed.
One fell off and the others said,
Would you please not shake the bed, Jed,
Would you please not shake the bed?

Two green turtles on a bed.
One fell off and the other said,
Would you please not shake the bed, Zed,
Would you please not shake the bed?

One green turtle on a bed.
One fell off and . . .

Eunice Meryl Was A Pretty Girl

Eunice Meryl was a pretty girl,
Oh, a pretty girl was she!
Loved her cats and loved her Lord
And loved her family,
Was so kind and good to all
That no one could deny
Everyone loved Eunice Meryl
And everyone knew why.

The Eyes Of Any Animal

The eyes of any animal
Will teach you what is true,
And if you look into them long
You'll know what's not true too.

Fairly Well, Thank Ye, Ma'am

Fairly well, thank ye, ma'am,
Fairly well I reckon.
I guess I'm doin fairly well
But my poor heart is peckin.
Peck! Peck! Peck! Peck!—
There she goes again.
If she don't get some better soon
I'll have to trade her in.

Purdy good, thank ye, sir,
Purdy good I'm thinkin.
I guess I'm doin purdy good
Though my poor eyes is blinkin.
Blink! Blink! Blink! Blink!—
There they go again.
If they don't cut that blinkin out
I'm tradin them things in.

Falstaff Was A Finch

Falstaff was a finch
In size about an inch
With a beak as red as scarlet thread
And a crow that made him flinch.

And outside on a bench
With a sweetheart that was French
He stuffed some bread into her head
And gave her wing a pinch.

Farmer Beanhead Had Two Dogs

Farmer Beanhead had two dogs
But that was two too many.
The way he treated those poor dogs
He shouldn't have had any.

Farmer Brown Had A Mule

Farmer Brown had a mule
And what a mule it was.
It smelled as fine as a Georgia pine
Or a honeysuckle does.
It had two ears and either ear
Was done up in a bow
With a yellow garter round one leg
I'd snap to make it go.
One eye was looking this away,
The other way off yonder.
But far from making me think less,
It made me that much fonder.
And oh how sweet that mule would grin
When I gave it a swaller
Of corn squeezings from the neighbor's
Down the path and up the holler.
And walking home together
I'd ride first then he'd climb on,
And we'd get home bout midnight
Before they ever knew we'd gone.

Fiddly, Fiddly, Foo

Fiddly, fiddly, foo,
I dunno what to do.
It's raining out,
It's boring in,
Fiddly, fiddly, foo.

Fiddly, fiddly, foe,
I wish the rain'd go.
Drip, drop!
Drop, drip!
Fiddly, fiddly, foe.

Fiddly, fiddly, fink,
It looks like I might sink.
Buttleup!
Burgle! Burp!
Fiddly, fiddly, fink.

The Fields Are White With Snow

The fields are white with snow;
I'm glad to say it's so.
If there were any green I'd know,
But the fields are white with snow.

I'll put my snowshoes on
Before the snow is gone;
I can walk across my father's lawn
If I put my snowshoes on.

And I'll wear my furry hat
With a tail just like a cat.
Cause you can see where I am at
If I wear my furry hat.

And I'll wrap up really good
Like mother says I should;
In the wintertime it's understood
That I wrap up really good.

And I'll march out in the snow
Just like an Eskimo;
Till I'm too old and cold to go
I'll march out in the snow.

The Fish I Caught Was Sort Of Little

The fish I caught was sort of little
Though it had a tummy in its middle,
A tummy yellow, white, and round
Just like the golf ball Daddy found.

A Flock Of Cows Went Flying By

A flock of cows went flying by
And blocked the sun up in the sky
And it grew dark and rather cool
And all the teachers in the school
Decided they should cancel class
And let the students go to mass.
"The end is here!" one of them said,
And put a helmet on her head.
And so filled was she with agitation
She took an early spring vacation.
Left and right the teachers flew
Not knowing what on earth to do.
Frantically they chewed their lips
And grew clammy in their fingertips
And sweat poured down upon their brows—
Oh, how those teachers feared those cows!

A Fly And A Flea

A fly and a flea
Lit on a cat's knee
And commenced what they do with vigor.
What was that?! said the cat,
As he scratched where they were at,
A fly or a flea or a chigger?

Oh me, said the flea,
Did that chigger bother thee?
Oh my, said the fly, did he biteth, too?
We are poor wayfaring bugs
And those chiggers are such thugs.
I assure you, Brother Cat, we shall pray for you.

A Friar On A Fence Post

A friar on a fence post
Praying for some crows
Once said to one who cawed like mad
"It's reason I suppose

To wonder why you caw so loud
Yet never say two words;
I guess you must be sorely tried,
Much more than other birds."

"I ain't tried at all, Friar Tuck,"
The crow then said in Greek,
"But you must learn the language
If you want to hear crows speak."

Frog Stew, Frog Stew

Frog stew, frog stew,
Nothing like a frog stew.
But what's the froggy's point of view?
Yikes! Lemme out!

Double cheese, double cheese,
Nothing like a double cheese.
But what is doubled if you please?
Yikes! Lemme out!

Gimme That Hoe Handle

Gimme that hoe handle,
I'll show you how to use it.
You put your back in it, boy,
If it takes you all night.
This garden's what we live on
And we don't want to lose it.
You put your heart in it, boy,
And you do the thing right.

God Made Animals To Teach Us Folks

God made animals to teach us folks
How to tell the real one from the hoax.

A Goldfish Named Sushi

A goldfish named Sushi
Was so bright she just knew she
Was descended from a school of starfish.
But when she found out
What starfish were about
She swore that she meant to say tarfish.

Gootchy, Gootchy, Gootchy Goo

Gootchy, gootchy, gootchy goo,
Tell your Daddy what to do.
Make him jump, make him spin,
Make him stick his tongue out then.

Make him bark, make him quack,
Make him hurt his aching back.
Make him laugh, make him cry,
Make him sing a lullaby.

Make him get down on all-fours,
Make him open all the doors.
Make him hurt, make him pay,
Put him in his grave some day.

Got A Pork Chop In My Ear, Ear

Got a pork chop in my ear, ear;
Got a pork chop in my ear.
It's so hard to hardly hear
With a pork chop in my ear.

Got a carrot in my nose, nose;
Got a carrot in my nose.
It's so hard to smell a rose
With a carrot in my nose.

Got a finger in my nail, nail;
Got a finger in my nail.
It's so hard to pet a snail
With a finger in my nail.

Got a bumble in my bee, bee;
Got a bumble in my bee.
Shake it up and you will see
There's a bumble in my bee.

Got a dinosaur in my shoe, shoe;
Got a dinosaur in my shoe.
If I don't get that dinosaur out
I don't know what I'll do.

Granddaddy Longlegs, How I Wish

Granddaddy Longlegs, how I wish
You'd stay away from Luke's water dish.
Don't you know you cannot swim
And you can't drink as much as him!

Guess What Arnie Stepped In, You All

Guess what Arnie stepped in, you all—
Guess what Arnie stepped in.
If he stepped in a hole
I could reach him with a pole,
But Arnie didn't step in a hole.

And it doesn't smell like a rose, you all,
It doesn't smell like a rose.
If it smelled like a rose
I could stand it in my nose,
But it doesn't smell like a rose.

"Help! Help!" Cousin Todd Said

"Help! Help!" Cousin Todd said,
"I got hair upon my head!"
But his mom it did not bother—
"You just caught it from your father."

A Herd Of Meat Loaf On A Hill

A herd of meat loaf on a hill
Between a rock and a daffodil
Is as fair a sight as you will see
Unless it were a donut tree.

Here Lies Yokel Farnsworth

Here lies Yokel Farnsworth,
A man who did what he does,
Who once saw the sun rise
But forgot where it was.

Hey, Mama, Come Look

Hey, Mama, come look
What's on my leg,
I sat down on a rooster egg!

And the Mama rooster
And the Daddy hen
Plucked every feather off my chin!

And the chicken crowed
And the crow did roost
And the rooster squawked like a duck and goose!

Mama, I swear
That's how it was,
That's how them mother roosters does!

High Water! High Water!

High water! High water!
Water everywhere!
Must have been a rainstorm
Though I wasn't there.
I was in the desert
Wishing I could drink
From the rusty faucet
In my kitchen sink.

Hot sand! Hot sand!
Sand everywhere!
Must have been a sandstorm
Though I wasn't there.
I was in the ocean
Praying I could reach
A dry patch of hot sand
On the myrtle beach.

A Hippopotamule And A Gallonator

A hippopotamule and a gallonator
Swam up through an insulator
Looking for a place to dine.
Don't see one, said the gallonater,
Though I've pud in my optimator.
Did you bring the turpentine?

Oh blame, said the hippopotamule,
I left it in the motor pool.
I really must have lost my mind.
You lost the turpentine, said the gallonator,
But your mind's in the indicator
Of a little tail you trail behind.

I'd talk, said the hippopotamule.
If I had your restibule
I'd surely keep it free of pud.
Your tally ho's so over-waddled
You ought to have it diced and bottled
And then sold a dime a dud.

A Hog, A Frog, And A Dingbat

A hog, a frog, and a dingbat,
To keep from getting fat,
Vowed to eat mosquitoes for a year.

The frog gained two pounds nine;
The dingbat fared just fine;
The hog, it's said, did oddly disappear.

A Honeybee Kissed A Rose

A honeybee kissed a rose
Right upon the nose,
And the shock of it went to her toes
When a honeybee kissed a rose.

A rose kissed a breeze
Right there in the trees,
And it shocked her so it made her sneeze
When a rose kissed a breeze.

A breeze kissed a creek
Right upon the cheek,
And it shook so much it sprung a leak
When a breeze kissed a creek.

A creek kissed a lake
Which said for heaven's sake,
And it began to shift and shake
When a creek kissed a lake.

A lake kissed a sea
Which said you startled me,
But the waves reacted passively
When a lake kissed a sea.

A sea kissed the sand
Which took it by the hand,
And turned it into fertile land
When a sea kissed the sand.

A Hopper And A Crawler Tried

A hopper and a crawler tried
To get into a milk cow's hide
But when they found a likely spot
The milk cow thought they better not
And wading out into a pond
She licked them till their heads were gone.

The Hound In The Middle

The hound in the middle
Was a fine old hound
With hound dog ears
That hung to the ground.

The hound on the left
Was a stone-still hound
That made not even
One hound sound.

The hound on the right
Was a right good hound
With a right good
Hound dog look all around.

The hound on the top
Was a fairly round hound
With eyes in its head
That could not be found.

The hound on the bottom
Was a boring hound
Whose boring traits
Did quite abound.

The hound in the front
Was your average hound
With its mouth all slack
And its tongue unwound.

The hound in the back
Was a bashful hound
Whose heart kept going
Pound, pound, pound!

How Did Miss Tawdry Come To Be

How did Miss Tawdry come to be
As blue as any blue can be?—

Blue ears, blue nose, blue feet, blue toes,
Blue even in her panty hose,

Blue on top, blue in the britches,
Blue on the back, blue where it itches,

Blue on blue, both house and car,
A little blue pet, a blue guitar,

A little blue cup, a little blue glass,
A little blue fence, a little blue grass.

I asked Miss Tawdry why that's so
And she said I don't need to know,

So I put my red hat on my head
And went home to my little red bed.

How Many Gooses

How many gooses
Could lay three eggs
If a goose had a noose
Around both back legs?

Or how many chickens
Could duck one goose
If the noose on his legs
Somehow worked loose?

Or how big a goose
Would it take to find
One big feather
On her big behind?

Or how does one geese
When it is a gander
Put up with a goose
When he can't stand her?

Huggy Buggy Was A Bear

Huggy Buggy was a bear,
Hugged a bug was barely there.

When the bear did hug a-plenty
Bug was barely hardly any.

When he hugged it once too great
Bug did frankly dissipate.

Uh-oh, Huggy Buggy sigh,
And went to hug a butterfly.

Human Beans Is More Intilligent

Human beans is more intilligint
Then most all other creetures.
They read and stuff and calcolate
And sometimes become teechers.

And if there really good at it
I learn to sound it out
Or speel it close enough for them
Which what's life all about.

It don't matter what I say
As long as my hart's in it
And she can git the thrust of it
Just how I really ment it.

And if I tell it good enough
She'll tape it to the dore
And I can show my mom and pop
And they won't kuss no more.

Hurry, Hurry, Come And See

Hurry, hurry, come and see—
She's running up the road!
The basketball is spit-shined
And my hands are icy cold.
We'll dribble it upon the snow
And shoot just like Bob Cousy
And if I beat Aunt Temple twice,
She'll know I am a doozy.
A doozy, boyz, a doozy, girlz,
And I don't ever loozy.
And if I beat Aunt Temple twice
She'll know I am a doozy.

I Ain't A-Goin A Go To Town

I ain't a-goin a go to town,
I ain't a-goin a go.
I gonna sit here on the porch
And watch the garden grow.

Watch the garden grow, Ma,
Watch the garden grow.
I gonna sit here on the porch
And watch the garden grow.

I ain't a-goin a go to work,
I ain't a-goin go.
I gonna sit here on the porch
And watch the garden grow.

Watch the garden grow, Ma,
Until it's fully grown.
I gonna sit here on the porch
As if it was my own.

I ain't a-goin a go to church,
I ain't a-goin a go.
I gonna sit here on the porch
And watch the river flow.

Watch the river flow, Ma,
Watch the river flow.
I gonna sit here on the porch
And watch the river flow.

I ain't a-goin a pray, Ma,
I ain't a-goin a pray.
I gonna sit here on the porch
Until the judgment day.

Until the judgment day, Ma,
Until the judgment day.
I gonna sit here on the porch
Until the judgment day.

I Ate A Chicken

I ate a chicken
Which was pretty tough,
But them dadburn feathers
Were bad enough.
They got in my nose,
They got in my ears,
They got in my eyes
And brought the tears.
They got in my mouth
And I swallowed hard,
Then went to peckin'
Around the yard,
Cluckin' and scratchin'
Like a mother hen,
Up one side and down again.

I Climbed A Mountain Great And Tall

I climbed a mountain great and tall
And had a great and mighty fall

And climbed again and fell again
And might have ceased to climb at all

But for the urgings of a friend
And my own discontent within.

In other words, I made me sick
Till someone gave my *ummph* a kick!

If A Fish Doesn't Swim

If a fish doesn't swim
I wonder what it is.
Still a fish I would wish
But that's none of my biz.

If An Ear Was A Nose

If an ear was a nose
We would smother I suppose,
But everything we'd smell
We could hear it very well.

If I Stand On My Head

If I stand on my head,
Will you? Will you?
If I stand on my head,
Will you?

Did you hear what I said?
If I stand on my head,
Will you? Will you?
Will you?

If I stand on my feet,
Will you? Will you?
If I stand on my feet,
Will you?

Do I have to repeat
If I stand on my feet,
Will you? Will you?
Will you?

If I Was A Cowboy I'd

If I was a cowboy I'd
Lasso something far and wide;

I'd lasso left, I'd lasso right,
I'd sometimes lasso day and night;

I'd lasso high, I'd lasso low,
I'd lasso places I don't know;

I'd lasso big, I'd lasso little,
I'd lasso some right in the middle;

I'd lasso north, I'd lasso south,
I'd lasso even with my mouth;

I'd lasso in the family car,
I'd lasso in the pickle jar;

I'd lasso in the easy chair,
I'd lasso in my underwear;

I'd lasso beef, I'd lasso jerky,
I'd lasso ham, I'd lasso turkey;

I'd lasso skipping to my lou,
I'd lasso doing number two;

I'd lasso sleeping in my bed;
I'd lasso standing on my head;

I'd lasso teachers, preachers, crooks;
I'd lasso clerks, I'd lasso cooks;

I'd lasso dogs and cats and fleas,
I'd lasso rocks, I'd lasso trees;

I'd lasso everywhere I went,
I'd be the lasso president.

Yes, if I was a cowboy I'd
Lasso till the day I died.

If I Was A Dog I Would Be One

If I was a dog I would be one,
Not just when I happened to see one.

If What You Want Is Mutton

If what you want is mutton
There's nuttin like a sheep,
But if what you want is crow's feet
Don't lay around and sleep.

If You're Lookin To Locate A Giant

If you're lookin to locate a giant,
I know where there might be a client.
He's about 8 feet 4 from his scalp to the floor
But his huge disposition's compliant.

You can take him wherever you're goin,
Though you barely come up to his groin.
It's really uncanny how he'll follow your fanny.
In fact he's so meek it's annoyin.

I Got Toes On My Feet

I got toes on my feet!
Well, what do you know.
I wonder how many will finally grow.
Ten so far but I am still a kid.
Bet I grow more than my Daddy did.

I got hairs on my head.
Well, that beats all.
I guess they'll disappear when I get tall.
Daddy's bald head shot right through his,
But I don't have to wonder where mine is.

I got fat on my belly.
Well, that's okay.
It'll keep me warm on a cold, cold day.
Daddy's got a belly, am I right or wrong?
Bet he stays hot nearly all year long.

I Had A Frog Named Freda

I had a frog named Freda,
A pale green senorita,
With skin as soft as Betty Lou
And legs just like a model.
But every time I hugged her
I guess it must have bugged her
Cause up she'd hop and never stop
Until she found a puddle.

I Heard A Bird When It Chirped On A Limb

I heard a bird when it chirped on a limb,
And I wondered what is it with himb.
He's always so sappy
And sounding so happy
There's no time that bird's feeling grimb!

I Knew A Bull With A New Gnu

I knew a bull with a new gnu
Diddly doo, diddly doo
Dressed up in a tutu
Diddly doo amore.

She was a new gnu who
Diddly doo, diddly do
Danced good as you do
Diddly doo amore.

And the bull danced some too
Diddly doo, diddly do
And together they flew
Diddly doo amore.

And while one would moo
Diddly doo, diddly doo
The other would woo
Diddly doo amore.

And often in May
Diddly doo, diddly doo
The new gnus will play
Diddly doo amore.

I Knew A Horse What Neighed So Silly

I knew a horse what neighed so silly
Everybody called him filly.
But then the fillies took offense
So he's been horsy ever since.

I Knew A Man Was Poor

I knew a man was poor,
Though I forget what for.
He had hands and feet
And meat to eat
And a ceiling and a floor.
Of that, I won't say more.

I knew a man was rich.
In what I can't say which.
He had no love
But from above
And no friend came to call.
He just stared at the wall.

I Met A Girl From Wales

I met a girl from Wales
Who loved to do her nails.
She'd trim and cut and file and chew
And curl her pointed claws at you
And grin just like a banshee do
Each time she did her nails.

I Met A Lady Running For Judge

I met a lady running for judge.
I said get away but she'd not budge.
She just stood there shaking my hand
And shook so hard it beat the band.
And grinning like a big old horse
She marched me down to vote of course
And showed me where to put my X,
Then smacked the man that walked by next.

I'm Going Out To Plant Me

I'm going out to plant me
A pocketful of wishes,
A sack full of chocolate
Fertilized with fishes.
And just like a pilgrim
I will grow my hair
While waiting for my chocolate tree
To shoot up in the air.

Chocolate sandwich,
Chocolate spread,
Chocolate chips
And chocolate bread,
Chocolate for everyone,
Even some for you,
And then I'll plant a ketchup tree
And make it chocolate too.

In Frenchburg Was A Foo

In Frenchburg was a Foo
Who looked just like a Fomp,
And everywhere he do
He said "Kerplomp! Kerplomp!"

And all the way to Rome
And halfway round Gibralter
He said "Kerplomp! Kerplomp!"
Then vanished in the walter.

In Lovely West Virginny

In lovely West Virginny
I bet D.D. a penny
I had found a shortcut
Through the mountains to Kaintuck.

And oh the road was skinny
And shapelier than many,
But down in D.D.'s gut
There was a fear he couldn't chuck.

Four hours passed, then five,
And the lovely mountain drive
Was not so very lovely
As it had been at the start.

For the darkness did arrive
And the trees did seem alive,
And the very air above me
Seemed oppressive to the heart.

Dark it got and darker
And stark it got and starker,
And D.D. got to chewing
On his toenails left and right.

Just a tourist or a parker
Or even one mile-marker
Would've made what was ensuing
Seem a little less a fright.

"Oh woe!" then D.D. muttered,
As at the windshield fluttered
A bat as white as cream
And near as silent as a cave.

And something else he uttered,
Though every word was stuttered,
As in our headlights' beam
Appeared a hut draped like a grave.

I hit the brakes and skidded,
Regretting that I did it,
For D.D. from the floor got up
As pale as grandma's sheet.

And his tongue he must have bit it
For between his teeth he slid it,
And spat into a cup
But spilled the contents on the seat.

And then he looked near dead,
As from the hut there up ahead
Came crawling a live body
That gave off an eerie glow.

"Don't move a lash," I said,
So D.D. moved his bowels instead,
And right there used the potty
Which, truth told, seemed apropos.

And then the figure stood,
And stood and stood and stood,
For up and up we saw it rise
Twelve feet or I'm a crazy.

We stared at what we could
But in the tangle of the wood
All we could see were hairy thighs
For above the waist was hazy.

"Hey, D.D., you still there?"
Said I into the air.
"I'm here," said he, "but I suspect
I'll split before you know it."

As a judgment that was fair,
For a crawling in my hair
On me had worked a like effect
Though I'd been slow to show it.

So I put the truck in scat
And right where we were at
Laid a patch of Goodyear
Which will be there when I'm brittle.

And with D.D. screaming that
We should run smack through the bat
I turned that four-wheel on its ear
And blew her out a little.

Inteleckshuls Is Smart

Inteleckshuls is smart
And think with their head
And like to say what
Dr. So-and-So said.
And if you disagree
They are taken aback,
Cause you're too dumb to see
How much data you lack.

In The Days When Time Was Older

In the days when time was older
And the inns so much the colder
And darkness that much darker
In the corners of a room

There lodged a fair young maiden
Whose heart was heavy laden
And her cold black eyes so stark her
Pretty face betrayed her gloom.

What was it made her wary?
And at her door latch tarry?
What was it in the bill she read
Or tried to read so oft?

And then quivering like a feather
While her teeth did jar together
She swooned against her quilty bed
And held the note aloft.

Oh, God, she cried, I'm done for.
And rushed back to the locked door
And looped the leather latch so tight
It broke in twos and threes.

God, help me! she intreated,
And the selfsame words repeated
When torches lit her window sash
And felled her to her knees.

Then round her was there howling
And footsteps outside prowling
And she though breathless tried to scream
But strength she lacked to do it.

And then an iron fist pounded
And horses' hooves resounded
And a cold blast from a bullock's horn
Went to her heart and through it.

What is it? said she fervent.
Your pizza! said the servant.
And knowing she was short two bits
Her knees began to give her fits.

I Piddle All Night

I piddle all night.
I piddle all day.
I piddle in the bed.
I piddle in the hay.

I piddle in the field.
I piddle in the pond.
I piddle in the church.
I piddle in the john.

I piddle in the tree.
I piddle on the ground.
I piddle head-first.
I piddle up and down.

I piddle like mad.
I piddle like crazy.
I piddle so much
I might be lazy!

I Saw A Snowman In A Field

I saw a snowman in a field,
Not so strange a sight,
Except that it was April
And it had rained all night.
I thought that he was lost
So I went to lend a hand,
And never have I seen
Such a sad and wasted man.
His arms were running down his sides
And his head had grown so little,
And a hole had started in his chest
That ate away his middle.
Tears from his eyes were streaming
And a lump in my throat grew,
For neither of us had a notion
What on earth to do.
Shorter he got, and thinner,
As if by some disease,
And just to look him in the eyes
I dropped down to my knees.
And right before he vanished,
I did all I could do—
I said, I love you, snowman.
Said he, I love you too.

I Sing Of Sweet, Sweet Julie

I sing of sweet, sweet Julie,
As fair as a petulley,
With hair the color of the hay
A little bit unruly.
I'd say she speaks as truly
As the sky above shines bluely
And though she's older every day
She always acts so newly.

I've Done All I Can Do

I've done all I can do.
Lord, now it's up to you.
The world can be so big and mean
And I am such a little thing.
I need someone who's tall
To help me through it all.

I've Got A Friend Who's Sort Of Neat

I've got a friend who's sort of neat
But he's got two big smelly feet.

One on the left, one on the right,
You'd think he'd keep them out of sight.

But every time he comes around,
There they are upon the ground.

That's bad enough but what is worse,
Before they're there, you smell them first.

I Will Remember By And By

I will remember by and by
When I see a yellow butterfly,
There never was a thing so free
As the little blonde curls of Cindy B.

I Will Sing While I Can

I will sing while I can,
Yes I will, yes I will.
I will sing while I can, Uncle Willie.
I will sing with all I've got,
I will sing until I'm not,
It's my calling and I will surely do it.

I will sing while I live,
Yes I will, yes I will.
I will sing while I live, Uncle Willie.
And when I disappear
All my songs will still be here.
It's my calling but no one ever knew it.

Jerry Jumped A June Bug

Jerry jumped a June bug
While hunting in the yard,

And said then, "Stick 'em up, ol' buzz,
Or you'll go down real hard.

I'm the toughest hombre
This side of the street,

And if you give me any lip
I'll make you smell my feet."

And so the June bug stuck em' up
And lived to see the sunrise,

Cause Jerry found the jar was filled
With ladybugs and fireflies.

John Allen Shot A BB

John Allen shot a BB
Up into the air,

And there a crow did swallow it
And straight flew off somewhere.

And then one day for breakfast,
When John was having crow,

He bit down on that BB
So hard he broke a toe.

John Took His Retainer Out To Eat

John took his retainer out to eat
Down at the corner Hocks & Feet.
John had drits,
The retainer dravy,
After which they joined the navy.

Forty nights and days they sailed
But just outside of Greece they bailed.
John got drenched,
The retainer drippy,
After which they met a hippie.

All on foot they skipped along
Until the hippie sang a song.
Then John was droll,
The retainer drowsy,
After which they felt quite lousy.

Judge Poop Went Up An Alpine

Judge Poop went up an Alpine
Strutting straight and tall,
But came back down it supine,
Embarrassed by it all.

Kendall Was A Dribbler

Kendall was a dribbler
Who dribbled night and day,
Who dribbled up and down the street,
Who dribbled on the way,
Who dribbled down between his legs,
Who dribbled on his head,
Who dribbled in the back seat,
Who dribbled in the bed,
Who dribbled with his fingers,
Who dribbled with his toes,
Who dribbled with his elbow,
Who dribbled with his nose,
Who dribbled in the schoolhouse,
Who dribbled in detention,
Who dribbled nearly everywhere
Too numerous to mention.
And when he tried to take a nap
He dribbled in his sleep,
And got a decent scholarship
To dribble bouncing sheep.

Kentucky Is My Favorite Country

Kentucky is my favorite country
Long bout 6 A.M.

The sun comes up above the tree
With me there on the limb.

And I let her go and start to crow
From then till long bout noon.

Then I let her rest to be my best
A-crowin at the moon.

Kimberly Brent Was Famed For His Knack

Kimberly Brent was famed for his knack
Of pulling a tick from a hounddog's back.
He'd tickle its feet and when it let go to scratch
He'd light up its head with a kitchen match.

Kittyhawk, You Fly It

Kittyhawk, you fly it,
And like a crow I'll try it.
If I can't fly from tree to tree
I'll have to fly from sea to sea
To places I've not known
Until I've finally flown.

The Latest Dance Is The Crow-Walk

The latest dance is the crow-walk,
The latest talk is the crow-talk,
And if you can crow,
Then bless my soul,
Your social life is good to go!

Listen My Pods, You Peel The Peelings

Listen my pods, you peel the peelings
And I'll mash the tadas and wash the reelings
And Jode will tell the time is ticking
And Boob shall comb her hair.

And Boob shall comb her hair
And Jode will wish her fair
And I'll be belling the bells all clicking
And everyone will there.

And everyone will there
And what we don't we'll wear
And when the day is gone forever
I will sing we were and never
See the three of us together
'Cept it be in air.
'Cept it be in air.

Little Boy Remember

Little boy remember
When you are old and gray
You never knew so much as when
You knew how to play.

Little Davy Got A Banjo

Little Davy got a banjo
And he played it mighty thick;
Then he played it like a feather;
Then he played it like a stick;

Then he played it like a hammer;
Then he played it like a bell;
Then he played it like a banjo,
And we all said, "Do tell."

Little Mouse, Little Mouse

Little mouse, little mouse,
Living in a little house,
How did you come to be
Before you came to be with me?

Were you just as poor?
And did you know what life was for?
And did you wonder who
Made me me and made you you?

Loan Me A Dollar, Jeff

Loan me a dollar, Jeff,
Will ya, huh? Will ya, huh?
Loan me a dollar, Jeff,
So I can buy a posy.

Loan me another, Jeff,
Will ya, huh? Will ya, huh?
Loan me another, Jeff,
Cause two is much more cozy.

Loan me a third, Jeff,
Will ya, huh? Will ya, huh?
Loan me a third, Jeff,
And don't you be so nosey.

Lord, Bless The Sun That's Full Of Crows

Lord, bless the sun that's full of crows
And bless the moon nobody knows,
And bless the wind and bless the rain
And bless my dirty windowpane.
And bless the bug that's on my ear
And bless the fate that brought it here.

Mama Gimme Some Dem Dar Soup Bean

Mama gimme some dem dar soup bean
And some dem cornbread and some dem green,

And some dem fry tada and country ham
And some dem butter and some dem jam.

Mama put all dem dar on my plate
And I be most appreciate.

Mamaw Loved Her Parakeet

Mamaw loved her parakeet,
Loved its head and pair of feet,
Loved its feather, loved its wing,
Loved it like no other thing,
Loved it cause it sang so sweet
And loved when Mamaw sang "Tweet, tweet."

Mary, Mary, If You Will Work

Mary, Mary, if you will work,
For what will you work, Mary Mahler?

I will work, Steve Cope, for money I hope.
I will work, Steve Cope, for a dollar.

A dollar it is then, and if you do well,
I will hire you next week and thereafter.

Then I won't eat your fish and break every dish
And swing by my heels from your rafter.

Menifee, Menifee

Menifee, Menifee,
Goin back to Menifee—
No more clocks, locks, and traffic jams
In this life for me.
Tell the girl with the nose-ring
She can have my TV.
Got the earth for diversion in Menifee.

Menifee, Menifee,
Send my mail to Menifee,
And I'll send back my answer
On a fast honeybee.
I'll tie a string to its whisker
And sail it to thee,
Then reel it back home to Menifee.

A Miss Cleaver Of Harvard

A Miss Cleaver of Harvard
With eyes a bit starboard
And skin just as yellow as cornbread

And hair of the kind
That stood straight up behind
If she lay on her back in her dorm bed

Was a studious sort
Who would sometimes resort
To the bookroom to sign out a novel,

And that's where she met
(Day or night I forget)
A bookworm there known as Is-TA-bul.

Now Is-TA-bul was slim
And had a ring around him
That made him look much like a pencil.

So that's why, someone said,
She sharpened his head:
She thought him a writing utensil.

A Moo And A Bow Wow

A moo and a bow wow
I really don't know how how
Looking for a paw paw
Fell into a pond.

Help! cried the moo.
Help! cried the bow wow.
Then they heard a caw caw
Coming from beyond.

What?! said the caw caw
To the moo and bow wow,
And to the ground he flew flew
And on it sat upon.

What?! said the caw caw,
What am I to do do?
I am just too few few
And you must weigh a ton.

And so the moo and bow wow
Sank into the wa wa
And never found a paw paw
This side of the sun.

A Mosquito With A Tiny Buzz

A mosquito with a tiny buzz
To find out what an echo was
Buzzed into a hollow tree
As loud as loud for him could be.

'Pon my honor, said a spider,
As he jumped right out to bite her,
I came here to meditat-tat-tat
And I don't have to deal with that!

Mr. Bradshaw Had A Black Bull

Mr. Bradshaw had a black bull,
A black bull, a black bull.
Mr. Bradshaw had a black bull
And that black bull was hairy.

So we shaved off that black bull,
That black bull, that black bull.
So we shaved off that black bull
Till a hair he had nary.

Then he looked like a peeled grape,
A peeled grape, a peeled grape.
Then he looked like a peeled grape
Or some kind of berry.

So we got him a wighat,
A wighat, a wighat.
So we got him a wighat
And boy, did he look scary!

The Mud Is Standing In The Yard

The mud is standing in the yard;
It's much too wet to play.
The rain is coming down so hard
I've just got time to say:

I love you little Susan,
Janie and Shelley too.
And when the years have come and gone
I'll still be loving you.

My Cat Killed My Bird

My cat killed my bird
And I cried and cried

And thought now I know
Why my Jesus died.

I hurt so much
I took a nap

With that murdering cat
Curled up on my lap.

My Mama Had Three Brothers

My mama had three brothers;
Each one looked like the others.
They wooed the sweetest girls around
And drove them twice across the town
And thought it time to settle down
And turn them into mothers.

My Mama Had Three Sisters

My mama had three sisters,
Who every one had blisters.
They'd hoe the corn which wasn't fair
And go back home to roll their hair
And cool off in their underwear
And talk about their misters.

Napples And Urnges

Napples and urnges,
Nanas and drapes,
All sorts of colors
And all sorts of shapes,

All sorts of flavors
For fruity fruit freaks,
But God made the lemon
To pucker your cheeks.

To pucker your cheeks,
That's what it's for—
Till you look like a fish
On the blue ocean floor.

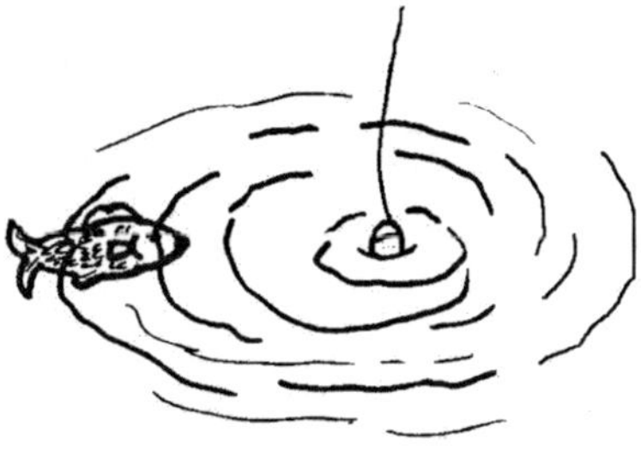

Never Was There A More Fickle

Never was there a more fickle
Teacher than a Mr. Bickle,
With green ears on his head
And a nose that was said
To run when it had just a tickle.

And as there appeared just a trickle,
I bet my good buddy a nickel
That before he could say
His fever was hay
His nose would turn green as a pickle.

No Child Is Less, No Child Is More

No child is less, no child is more,
But every child can say what life is for.

It's for watching the sun come up over a hill,
And the moon and the stars and the whippoorwill.

It's for drinking and tasting and smelling it all,
It's for seeing and hearing and throwing a ball,

And touching and feeling the dirt and the soap,
And running like crazy and jumping a rope.

It's for kissing your mama and hugging your dad,
And feeling the pain of the guilt when you're bad.

No child knows less, no child knows more,
But every child knows what this life is for.

Nothing Compares With A Do-Dilly-Deer

Nothing compares with a Do-Dilly-Deer,
With a hump on its back and a bug in its ear,
And some grass in its mouth and a smile on its face
And polka-dot freckles all over the place,
And a beard on its chin and hair on its knees
And its coat populated with chiggers and fleas,
And two toes on each foot tied up in a knot
And a wig hat that flutters when it starts to trot,
And twenty-three teeth straight across in a row
And a curly-cue tail that it carries in tow,
And sort of an antler on top of its head
And a couple of feathers, one green and one red,
And whiskers as stiff as a porcupine quill
And a horse fly that buzzes around its orange bill,
And a pink tongue that dangles and whips back and forth
And one wiry eyebrow that's pointed due north,
And headlights that shine wherever it goes
And blue fog that erupts from the end of its nose,
And if you smell something when something's not here,
That's a very good sign it's a Do-Dilly-Deer.

Of All The Waddlings In The Creek

Of all the waddlings in the creek,
There was this one could not but squeak,
And then its mother circling back
Went to claim her baby quack.

Oh The Winter Is Over

Oh the winter is over
And the springtime is here.
It's time for the buds
On the trees to appear.

It's time to go wading
And time for short pants,
Time for the flies
And the bees and the ants.

It's time to go camping
And time to pick flowers,
Time for warm nights
And the long daylight hours.

It's time for the birds
And the rabbits and squirrels,
Time for the boys
To chase after the girls.

It's time to mow grass
And time to wash cars,
Time to lie on our backs
And gaze up at the stars.

Oh the winter is over
And though I love the snow,
I love the spring
More than you'll ever know.

Old Bullet Was A Good Old Dog

Old Bullet was a good old dog
If ever I did see one;
There never was a better dog
And never gonna be one.

He barked the cars from dark till dawn
To make sure they kept going;
Then slept the sleep of the innocent
With mamaw downstairs sewing.

Old Bummy Could Count To Ten

Old Bummy could count to ten
Without a single finger;
At least that's what he said,
Though certain doubts still linger.

Like one day as we played some golf
And had to keep a tally,
Why'd he take his golf shoes off
And with his toes did dally?

Once A Boy Did Not Know

Once a boy did not know
So he set out to learn,

And he learned that he had
What he never did earn.

And every rock, every tree,
Every winding country road

Taught him he knew
What he'd never been told.

Once Upon A Time A Bird Laid An Egg

Once upon a time a bird laid an egg,
Not so strange or so unique.
All sorts of birds lay eggs of all sorts,
But this one was an . . . EEEK!

It was ten times as big as its mother was,
Ten times as deep and wide,
Ten times as high, ten times as long,
Ten times as hard to hide.

It was polka-dotted everywhere
With yellow, green, and blue,
With a north pole right on top of it
And a south pole on it too.

It weighed so much it soon began
To bend the tree branch down
Until the egg slipped from the nest
And sailed off toward the ground.

And bounding like a rubber ball
It bounced and rolled and twisted
Right through a crowded city street
Where cars just barely missed it.

Oh! Eeeeek! the mother bird exclaimed.
Don't look! her husband crowed.
For he saw the thing was hatching
In the middle of the road.

The horns began to toot and blow
When the egg began to crack.
The other birds flew for their lives
Too frightened to look back.

So what was it in that giant shell
That caused such great commotion?
Nobody knows for when it hatched
It flew into the ocean.

One Day Uncle Owen

One day Uncle Owen
To the barn was a-goin
When all of a sudden he saw

A spider on a milkweed
Long-legged and knock-kneed
Eating a honeybee raw.

Delicious, it said,
And rubbed its bald head
And curled up its tongue like a claw.

And Uncle Owen admitted
Though he didn't say quit it
He wished there was some kind of law.

Ophelia Was A White Bird

Ophelia was a white bird,
An itty bitty white bird,
A tiny hiny white bird
That thought she was a crow.

And every time she crowed some,
Closed her eyes and crowed some,
Braced her heels and crowed some,
The crows would say, Oh no!

She's gonna blow again, boys!
Gonna squeak again, boys!
Plug your ears again, boys!
She's gonna let it go!

Our Homerun Fence Was A Telephone Wire

Our homerun fence was a telephone wire
And I hit that ball so high
It smacked a buzzard up side the head
And we thought that thing would die.

It made a couple of sputtering starts
Then coughed and stalled somewhat
And Kitty and Brenda and Diane and Cheryl
All fainted on the spot.

And John came running with a sack
To catch it when it fell
And Ronnie and Tommy who knew first-aid
Read the situation well.

They sent out Marcus for some masking tape
And Victor for some salve
And Jerry for some splints and stuff
Or whatever he might have.

And Cliff pulled out a band-aid
And Bobby found some gauze,
And Vernon caught a doodlebug
To contribute to the cause.

And Vaughn said he had something,
And Pam and Ellen too,
And Mark and Carolyn ran for pills,
And Mike called up the zoo.

And Janet C. and Julie
Told David to find Dad
And Steve and O.V. bounced around
And Linda looked so sad.

And Jay Jay cleaned his glasses
And Kathy bit her lip
And Mary Lou and Sandy
Put a hand upon each hip.

And David P. and Nancy H.
Said Bob and Bud would do
To go get this or that or those
At the PDQ.

And Mickey found an aspirin
And Cassie held her nose
And Lisa ran around a tree
And Ricky struck a pose.

And Judith brought a blanket
And Jennifer plopped down
And turned a somersault so fast
Her diaper came unwound.

And Carlos, Louie, and Lois
Set a roadblock on home plate
Cause the buzzard was descending
At a meteoric rate.

Its feathers were in disarray
And its tongue hung out so far
That we could see it from the earth
Much clearer than a star.

Like a rocket coming in
It whistled as it dropped
But just two inches from the ground
It suddenly just stopped.

And revving up its motor
It taxied round the bases
And then took off into the sun
I guess toward other places.

Out In The Red Clover
Where Junior Bent Over

Out in the red clover where Junior bent over
And the billy goat grazed on the hill
I had a quick premonition that Junior's position
Would make one of them very ill.

Well, I tool a swaller and commenced to holler
Cause I felt in my heart it was fate
That made Junior bend over in that field of clover
As if he were fishing with bait.

Now I've been to Dallas and courted sweet Alice
And had steak and eggs down at Frisch's,
But I must admit just as sure as I sit
That I've not seen a goat so ambitious.

He reared like a horse (as a goat will of course)
And lowered his head with conviction
And shot like a rocket at Junior's back pocket
And I think I saw sparks from the friction.

Now I can't remember—was it May or Juvember?—
When Junior got back on his feet.
But I've never seen (I don't mean to be mean)
A change in a man so complete.

While he used to be cocky (he was built just like Rocky!)
Now he's as meek as a sheep
And won't go to bed without feeling some dread
That he might just get rammed in his sleep.

Pammy Had A Mammy Good As Pure Gold

Pammy had a mammy good as pure gold
And Pammy had a daddy that never got old.
Never got old, never got old,
Pammy had a daddy that never got old.

Pammy had a sister pretty as a rose
And Pammy had a daddy light on his toes.
Light on his toes, light on his toes,
Pammy had a daddy light on his toes.

Pammy had a cousin put words on a page
And Pammy had a daddy who knew how to age.
Knew how to age, knew how to age,
Pammy had a daddy who knew how to age.

Papaw Got Baptized In A Pond

Papaw got baptized in a pond
While Mamaw on the bank looked on,
And all the angels in the trees
Amen'd when they heard Papaw sneeze.

Papaw Had A Sweetheart

Papaw had a sweetheart
He loved with all his might,
And when he called her "Poodle,"
I knew it was all right.

Patty, Patty Picked A Pod

Patty, Patty picked a pod
Of peas and paid a-plenty.
Patty later lost her purse
That cost her quite a penny.
Patty after that was done
Did give the peas a pardon.
She set them free and then
Went all to pieces in the garden.

People Thinks Bats

People thinks bats
Is just flying rats,
But rats factually don't have the means.

In fact bats is rabbits
With all sorts of bad habits,
Like thinking their ears is wings.

A Polecat Is Not A Tadpole

A polecat is not a tadpole
But they are kin and that's a fact.
For the Lord gave to each one of them
A letter the other lacked.

Put A Hat On My Head So I Can Go

Put a hat on my head so I can go
Out in the rain where the wind might blow.
Then let it huff and puff and wheeze
And I'll just stand there in the breeze
And hear it whistle around my ears
And make my eyes fill up with tears.
And when I get back I'll tell you then
What it's like out in the wind.

Quit It, Said A Ferret

Quit it, said a ferret.
Quit what? said a cat.
Quit *that*, said a ferret.
That what? said a cat.
You know what, said a ferret.
What what? said a cat.

That what, said a ferret.
What that what? said a cat.
That that what, said a ferret.
What that that what? said a cat.
That that that what, said a ferret.
What that that that what? said a cat.

Ray's Tire Went Flat

Ray's tire went flat
As a pancake fritter
And he got out to change it
With the baby sitter.
Ray's jack broke
And set him a-cussin
And the babysitter blushed
And started fussin.
They screamed and hollered
Up and down the street
And Ray dropped a hammer
On the babysitter's feet.
She yelled murder
And the neighbors ran out
And somebody said,
What's this all about?
And the cops were called
And they came flying
Like they thought
Someone was dying.
They grabbed old Ray
By the end of the nose
And the fire truck came
With a water hose
And sprayed Ray down
And he started coughin
And somebody said
Does he do this often?
And somebody else said
I don't know about that,
But Ray goes crazy
When he has a flat.

A Rhinoceros Is Rather Crude

A rhinoceros is rather crude
Though good for digging ditches,
And the spot of tea he takes with me
Is worth a pair of britches.

But when he dons my overalls
And goes to plow the garden
I make him keep his plowshare hid
Or say I beg your pardon.

Rhyming Is Okay

Rhyming is okay
If one knows what to say.
And though one may not know it,
One might then be a poet.

One might rhyme his hat with cat
And some other things like that—
Dog with hog and dish with fish
And whatever one might wish,

Car with star and tick with brick,
One might even lick a stick,
Spot with hot and sun with fun,
Wing with sing and run with gun,

Shark with ark, eat with feet,
Rose with nose and sweet with wheat.
And if one wants to end the rhyme
One can do it any time.

Robin, Pray Tell Why You Chirp

Robin, pray tell why you chirp.
With all you eat it seems you'd burp!

Scarecrow, I'm Telling You

Scarecrow, I'm telling you,
Let those crows alone.
They'll just eat a little corn
And then they'll fly back home.

Scarecrow, I'm telling you,
You do what I said.
Or I'll take off that ugly hat
And plant corn upon your head.

Sir Dragon Danforth Had A Tail

Sir Dragon Danforth had a tail
That stretched from Georgia up to Maine,
And every time he did exhale,
They had to beg him to refrain.

Slim And Not So

Slim and Not So
Went on a date.
Slim went early,
Not So late.

Slim wore green,
Not So red.
Slim shaved his face,
Not So her head.

Slim wore pants,
Not So a dress.
Slim looked sharp,
Not So a mess.

Sim danced a lot,
Not So a little.
Slim shook his bottom,
Not So her middle.

Slim ate a steak,
Not So a crabtail.
Slim chipped a tooth,
Not So a toenail.

Slim got sick,
Not So sleepy.
Slim looked bad,
Not So creepy.

Slim said, "Well,
I'll see you when I'm better."
Not So said,
"I'd prefer a letter."

Someone Let The Cows Out

Someone let the cows out;
Now they're in the corn!
David run tell Papaw;
Julie, blow your horn!

Gary's in the hayloft;
Kim is on the pot;
Greg is playing checkers;
Jeff, I don't know what!

Wilma, go tell Mamaw;
And better do it quick;
Pick up on your way back
A good tobacco stick.

Patty, tie your dress up;
Wade out in the pond;
That bull is staring down that
Red sweater you got on.

Suuck, cow! Suuck, cow!
Get back where you should be.
Someone left the gate flung wide—
I hope it wasn't me!

Sometimes I Just Has To Laugh

Sometimes I just has to laugh,
So I laughs and laughs and laughs and laughs.
And when my friends ask what's so funny,
I just say the ether bunny.

Sometimes It Does

Sometimes it does.
Sometimes it doesn't.
Sometimes it was.
Sometimes it wasn't.

Sometimes it's funny,
Sometimes sad.
Sometimes good
And sometimes bad.

Sometimes it's boring,
Sometimes not.
Sometimes it takes
The whole parking lot.

But whatever's gonna
Happen will.
That's one thing you
Can count on, Bill.

Sometimes The Dumbest Of The Lot

Sometimes the dumbest of the lot
Will tell you plain what God forgot
And looking wisely into space
Reveal the mustard on his face.

So Said A Wise Man Upside-Down

So said a wise man upside-down
While peering up into the ground:
"The hardest thing in life to do,
Discern the truth from point-of-view."

So Tired I Am

So tired I am,
I mean way so,

Too way tired
To even go.

Too tired to stand,
Too tired to sit,

Too tired to even
Speak of it!

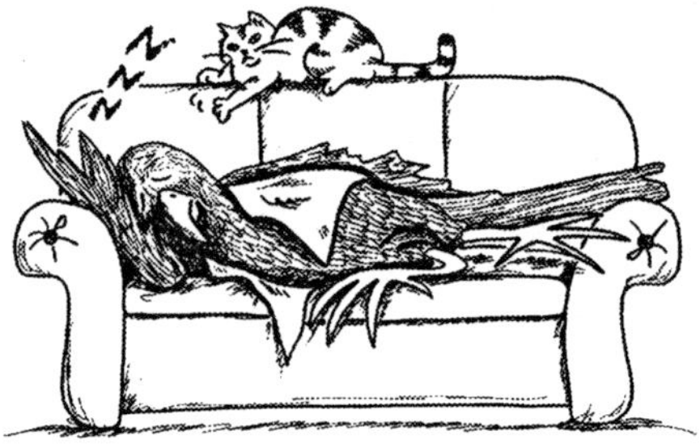

Spark Plug, Spark Plug

Spark Plug, Spark Plug,
Time to hit the trail;
We're gonna go fishing
With a crawdad tail.
Mama's had a baby
And Daddy's a wreck;
Gonna wade Glady Creek
Up to your neck.
Might catch a sunfish,
Might catch a bass,
Might catch a cold
Or a snake in the grass.
Might pull a red-eye
Out of the rocks,
Might find a June bug
Down in your socks.
Daddy might say,
There's a biggin over there!
And we might say,
Where Daddy? Daddy where?
Then Daddy might say,
Well, I could've been wrong.
Spark Plug, Spark Plug,
Get a move along.

Speaking Of Dogs, There's A Few That

Speaking of dogs, there's a few that
Have more fleas than you care to shoot at.
And though you are tough
And made of good stuff,
Boy, you wish they wouldn't do that!

Spunky And Luke Were A Right Rowdy Pair

Spunky and Luke were a right rowdy pair,
Until Spunky got out and ran off somewhere.
And it made Luke cry which was something rare—
Come home, Spunky, come home.

Come home, Spunky; Spunky, come home.
Life's too lonely to be alone.
Luke's going crazy by the telephone—
Come home, Spunky, come home!

Spunky's Back! Spunky's Back!

Spunky's back! Spunky's back!
Hallelujah, Spunky's back!
And old Steve's life is back on track.
And old Luke's back to his all-day snack.
We're oh so happy that Spunky's back.

Sycamore, Sycamore

Sycamore, sycamore,
Why'd they call you syca for?
Guess that if I had to pycka,
I'd say someone played a trycka.

A Teacher Knows A Thing Or Two

A teacher knows a thing or two,
One might as well admit it,
So when a child has found some joy
The teacher must say quit it.

Teacher,Teacher, Just Today

Teacher, teacher, just today
Let all of the children play.
Close the books and cap the pen;
Let the fun and games begin.

There's Nothing Quite So Peaceful

There's nothing quite so peaceful
As cattle in a field.
I know there's got to be in that
Some mystery revealed.

There Was A Bird

There was a bird
And there was a cat.
One looked like this,
The other that.

One had wings
And therefore flew.
One sat on the ground
And wanted to.

Tweet, tweet, the bird said.
Tweet, said the cat,
And flapped his paws
Till he fell down flat.

Up again, flap, flap,
Down again, Splat!
Up again, flap, flap,
He fell down flat.

But what would happen
If cats could fly?
Would cats by the truckload
Fill the sky?

Would they sit on wires
Till they weighed them down?
Would they perch like pigeons
On the eaves downtown?

Would they build their nests
In the tall, tall trees?
Would their wings buzz, buzz
Like honeybees?

Would they lay blue eggs
Like the robin does?
Would their babies forget
What a cat once was?

Around and around and around
The bird flies.
And the cat on the ground
Just cries and cries.

There Was A Crow Who Knew So Much

There was a crow who knew so much
He was sure to run you through it.
And though he never did it
He could tell you how to do it.

And when he spoke of anything
You'd think that he had made it,
And anyone who did good work
Was always overrated.

And if you did your very best
There'd surely be a flaw,
And he let you know it right away
With a condescending caw.

And though he'd never read a book
He could tell you how to write one.
And he acted like the king of beasts
Until he had to fight one.

There Was A Lion Not A King

There was a lion not a king
Who thought he wasn't anything,

Not a king, not a prince,
Not a kitten on a fence,

Not a truck and not a flea,
Not a line of poetry,

Not a man, not a boy,
Not a tool and not a toy,

Not a ball, not a box,
Not a wolf and not a fox,

Not a fish and not a fowl—
What was this lion anyhow?

There Was An Old Outhouse In Back

There was an old outhouse in back,
Oh wonderful welcome old shack,
Where philosophies were born
And pages were torn
And time was spent just keeping track.

With the sun coming in through a crack
And the lime lying there in a sack
A mud dauber would buzz
Or whatever it was
At a spider that I'd almost smack.

"Don't do it!" he blurted one day.
"You do it and you'll surely pay.
We spiders are ugly
And a little too bugly
But you treat me kind or I swear,
I'll get in your underwear . . ."

There Was A Poor Sap From Madrid

There was a poor sap from Madrid
Who thought that he probably did.
Or if he didn't he should've
And no doubt he would've
If they hadn't nailed down every lid.

There Was A What

There was a what
And there was a who
And both went up
To Kalamazoo.

And there they met
A when and where
Who showed up
In their underwear!

So what was what
And who to do—
Cry? Laugh?
Cheer? Boo?

They got a switch
And switched them good
As anybody's
Mommy would.

Though I Forget Now What It Was

Though I forget now what it was,
What happened's what usually does.
In fact it took place
At a horrible pace
And all that was left was the buzz.
Thus I forget now what it was.

Three Aardvarks Are In The Kitchen

Three aardvarks are in the kitchen
And Mama's got a broom;
I wonder if they'll live to tell it
Down at the Aardvark Room.

Three Cows Grazing

Three cows grazing
Calmly on a hill,
One ate a bumblebee
On a daffodil.

One called a doctor,
One called a priest,
One said "You all could fetch
The water trough at least!"

The Trees Outside Look Ghostly

The trees outside look ghostly
But what's scary to me mostly
Is the news on my TV
And people fighting constantly.

Lord, grant me peace and quiet
Far from war and riot,
And make all those who love such folly
Go to bed without their dolly.

Two-Dogs And Half-A-Dog

Two-Dogs and Half-A-Dog
Made a bow and arrow
And tried to slip between two rocks
But the path was narrow.

And so it happened Two got stuck
And Half-A-Dog did pray
Oh Lord forgive us what we made
And set Two free today.

And while he begged with all his might
For mercy to shine through,
Two-Dogs waited patiently
To lose a pound or two.

Uncle Jimmy Was A Good Man

Uncle Jimmy was a good man
Who worked hard all his life
And never said a dirty word
Or never beat his wife,
But never had a bird dog
Worth a chamber pot.
That's the truth, ain't it, Jimmy?
Just tell me that it's not.

Up

Up,
Then left,
Then right,
There we go.
Shake a finger,
Stump a toe,
Grab a partner,
Dosey-do.

Turn left,
Buckle those,
Heel to heel,
Nose to nose.
Turn a flip,
Duck a mole,
Throw your partner
Down a hole.

Back around,
Go to town,
Come back,
Quack quack.
Lift a knee,
Tie a shoe,
Tell your partner
What to do.

Climb a tree,
Scratch a flea,
Twist it off,
Stop and cough.
Go in,
Say hello,
Grab a partner,
Dosey-do.

Very, Very, Very Much

Very, very, very much,
Said a child with a crutch,
I wish I had your legs a while.
I'd go running for a mile.

You may borrow mine, I said,
For all day long I've been in bed;
All day long I've watched TV
While Mama brought my meals to me.

That's so sad, the child cried,
I thought you had been outside!
And taking my hand tenderly
She vowed to keep me company.

Wally Whoopee Found A Penny

Wally Whoopee found a penny
Hid beneath his bed,
And every time he thought of it,
Wally Whoopee said,

I love my penny, oh I do,
I love it like a dollar,
And every time I think of it,
It makes me want to holler.

Wahoo! Wahoo!
I hid it long ago,
And I forgot just where it was
But now I surely know!

Wahoo! Wahoo!
I searched high and low,
Cause I forgot just where it was
Until a while ago!

Whales Are Good If You Like Big

Whales are good if you like big,
And so is a pig.
But if you're looking for little,
They're not worth a fig.

What Mama Cooked The Children Ate

What Mama cooked the children ate
And left no crumbs upon their plate.
But when she came to sweep the floor . . .
Uh—oh!

When A Boy Goes Fishing It Is With One Wish

When a boy goes fishing it is with one wish,
That he catch the very biggest of the biggest fish.

Bass or sunfish, crappie or trout—
That's what he's after when the boat pulls out.

So he takes his pole and he takes his hook
And he takes new line and his record book,

And a can of curly worms to lure the big fish in,
And he's sure he'll catch it—he just can't say when.

So cast number one hooks a sycamore limb,
Cast number two snags a ragweed stem,

Cast number three snares a five-pound root,
Cast number four lands a size-12 boot,

Cast number five wraps around his pole,
Cast number six and he's ready to go,

He quits on seven so he won't know fate
Had a big bass waiting for cast number eight.

When I Get Too Hot It Is Odd

When I get too hot it is odd
How water comes out of my bod.
It flows down my temples
And onto my dimples—
Do you reckon that happens to God?

When I Was Just A Little Tad

When I was just a little tad
We bought a new Bumthrottle Pad

And shined it up to look like new
And splashed it with a dab or two

And built some legs and funny feet
And stood it upright on its tweet.

And then we wired it to the bed
And glued a hat upon its head

And stuck a feather in the hat
And thought it looked just fine like that.

And there it stood all day and night
Until we hid it out of sight

Cause sparks kept flying from its loon
And blocked the wottle of the moon.

I can't see it, Wilby said,
Turning over in his bed.

I can't neither! cried Bob Joe,
That crazy thing has got to go!

So we got up and drained its dwiddle
And parked it right behind the middle.

And now when we look way up high,
Bumthrottle sparks don't block the sky.

When Mr. Hunt Talks

When Mr. Hunt talks
Ron and Tom both listen,
And say of all the bad rules
Not one of them's this'n.

When Shep Were A Pup He Would Diddle

When Shep were a pup he would diddle
While the old men'd sit there and whittle
And spit on the fire or kick an old tire
Or an owlhoot'd play on his fiddle.
And a codger that bulged in the middle
Would tell them a real puzzling riddle,
And though they knowed what it meant
They would ack like they dint
And chew on their plug like a vittle.

Who'd A Thunk A Little Skunk

Who'd a thunk a little skunk
Would have a funky smell.

I bet you if it had a whiff
There'd be a tail for sell.

Whoever Said His Horse Did Neigh

Whoever said his horse did neigh
Must have said it from a sleigh.

Why Do Birdies Fly, My Mama?

Why do birdies fly, my Mama?
Why do birdies fly?

Because there is a sky, my daughter,
Because there is a sky.

Why do fishes swim, my Mama?
Why do fishes swim?

Cause it looks good on them, my daughter,
Cause it looks good on them.

Why do trees stand tall, my Mama?
Why do trees stand tall?

So they will not fall, my daughter,
So they will not fall.

Why are some bugs fat, my Mama?
Why are some bugs fat?

So you'll know where they're at, my daughter,
So you'll know where they're at.

Why are boxes square, my Mama?
Why are boxes square?

So they'll sit right there, my daughter,
So they'll sit right there.

Why is water wet, my Mama?
Why is water wet?

Because it's not dried yet, my daughter,
Because it's not dried yet.

Why is dark not light, my Mama?
Why is dark not light?

Then night would be too bright, my daughter,
Then night would be too bright.

Why do preachers pray, my Mama?
Why do preachers pray?

Because that is their way, my daughter,
Because that is their way.

Why do I want to know, my Mama?
Why do I want to know?

Because God made you so, my daughter,
Because God made you so.

Why You Gotta Do That, Do That, Do That?

Why you gotta do that, do that, do that?
Why you gotta do that—shake your dandruff out?

Every time you do that, do that, do that,
Every time you do that, I'm a-gonna shout

Why you gotta do that, do that, do that?
Why you gotta do that—shake your dandruff out?

Wild Dog Come Out Of Hiding

Wild dog come out of hiding,
What did you hope to see
When you sniffed the ground and looked around
And all you saw was me?

Wings Are Not Arms But They're Close

Wings are not arms but they're close,
As near as a pose to a post,
As an at to an it,
As a fight to a fit,
As an all might compare to almost.

Fingers aren't feathers it's true,
But as close as a seat to a pew,
As a tree to a stick,
As a tock to a tick,
As a me might compare to a you.

Willie And Junior And Jim

Willie and Junior and Jim—
There could not be a better them.
If I could pick three it might as well be
Willie and Junior and Jim.

A Wishy A Washy

A wishy a washy,
A wannabe too,
Stand up and show me
What you can do.

And do it with guts, child,
Do it with guts.
I don't want to hear
All your ands, ifs, and buts.

X Marks The Spot

X marks the spot,
Right there on the map,
Where Forrest carved the beech tree
And Owen took a nap,

And Charlie fished for crawdads
And the frogs came up to see
If he who turned the rocks on edge
Would be their destiny.

And Steven, John, and David
Stood above the falls
And looked down at the goings-on
And listened to the caws

Of crows up in the cornfield
And a barking dog somewhere,
And the peewees and the warblers
Sang and flitted through the air.

And Eunice Meryl and Temple
And Ruth and Wilma Jean
Picked wild flowers from the path
And dropped them in the stream.

And the flowers drifted slowly
Down the falls and through the swirls,
Where Papaw went to fish them out
For all the pretty girls.

One for Cindy, one for Sue,
One for Jane and Shelley too,
And one for Julie but the best
He pinned on Mamaw's yellow dress.

Yes And No Were Two

Yes and No were two,
One red the other blue,
Who used to walk
And used to talk
But now they seldom do.

Cause Yes said No was fat
And No called Yes a rat,
So Yes and No
Can hardly go
Together cause of that.

And when they chance to meet,
No looks at his feet,
And Yes looks at
His derby hat
And picks another seat.

And Yes is always sad
And No is feeling bad.
Which goes to show
That Yes and No
Did not know what they had.

You Got The Prettiest Black Coat

"You got the prettiest black coat
And the roughest rear-end
Of any cat a-goin or a-comin in.
But your old man's got a shiny head,"
So a friend of mine old D.D. said.

A Zit And A Zat

A zit and a zat
Upon a seaty sat,
And whatsoever Zit said
Zat said "Zowie."
So Zit said, "Zat,"
And Zat said, "Zowie,"
And Zit said, "I said Zat,"
And Zat said, "Zowie."
And Zit said, "This seaty's hot,
I think I'll find me one that's not,"
And Zat said, "Zowie!"
And Zit said, "Zat?"
And Zat said, "Zowie?"
And Zit said, "Are you okay?"
And Zat said, "Zowie."
And Zit said, "I saw a Sue,
And you know what she said of you?"
And Zat said "Zowie?"
And Zit said, "No,
She said that Zat is just so sweet,
A sweeter zat you'll never meet."
And Zat said, "Zoweeee!"

— The End —

Printed in the United States
71812LV00005B/1

9 781893 239364